BEYOND THE
BREAD BASKET

Editor's note: Yeast quantities are based
on standard U.S. packaging: i.e.,
active dry yeast is sold in 0.25-oz envelopes;
compressed fresh yeast is sold in 0.06-oz cakes.

With support from Lionel Pinot

Translated from the French by Carmella Abramowitz-Moreau
Design: Alice Leroy
Copyediting: Helen Woodhall
Proofreading: Chrisoula Petridis
Typesetting: Claude-Olivier Four
Color Separation: Turquoise, Emerainville, France

Distributed in North America by Rizzoli International Publications, Inc.

Originally published in French as *Autour des Pains d'Eric Kayser*
© Flammarion, Paris, 2007

English-language edition
© Flammarion, 2007

www.editions.flammarion.com

07 08 09 3 2 1
ISBN: 978-2-0803-0051-5

Dépôt légal: 02/2008
Printed in Singapore by Tien Wah Press

Eric Kayser

with Yaïr Yosefi

BEYOND THE BREAD BASKET

RECIPES FOR APPETIZERS, MAIN COURSES, AND DESSERTS

Photography by Clay McLachlan

Flammarion

Contents

Introduction

When you've grown up, as I did, in a family of bakers, it goes without saying that bread is an essential part of every meal. We ate bread in every conceivable form, both sweet and savory. Practically every day we would dip a crusty and pleasantly chewy piece of bread into a thick soup. I remember my father giving me a baguette hot out of the oven, the fresh butter melting into it.

All families of all origins have memories based on the simple pleasure that a good bread can give. Everyone has their own recipe for a favorite dish, which, together with bread, is a reminder of their childhood.

Ever since humans starting baking bread, they have incorporated other ingredients. In ancient times, the Greeks and Egyptians flavored their dough with olive oil or honey. The Romans dipped their bread in milk and eggs, the forerunner to our French toast. Later, in the Middle Ages, peasants survived on soup and cheese, essential complements to bread. The constraint seemed to be the need to have something to eat together with one's bread. But this was not always the case: in times of famine, peasants had to add earth and roots to their dough. Rest assured, I haven't included these recipes here.

I've taken some of my inspiration from historical recipes, and my travels across the world have given me other ideas for making and adapting breads. I've tasted and enjoyed Indian and eastern breads, often filled with vegetables, spices, and meat: pita filled with lamb to make a hot sandwich or cheese nan to attenuate the fiery spices of Indian cooking are just two examples. More intriguing, perhaps, are traditional Japanese ingredients such as seaweed, which I like to combine with rye.

For a balanced meal, you don't need to add much to bread. The recipes in this book should, for best results, be made with the freshest ingredients and the best quality bread. If you live far away from one of my bakeries, take the time to find a dedicated bread-maker, or use the recipes here to make your own bread.

I hope that you will enjoy sharing my memories, my travels, and my breads.

Eric Kayser

Good Bread Matters

Ingredients
(for 5 small loaves)

8 cups (1 kg) bread flour

2 ¼ cups (600 ml) water

1 tablespoon salt

⅓ envelope (2.5 g) active dry yeast or

⅓ cake compressed fresh yeast

(5 g fresh yeast); dissolved

in 4 tsp lukewarm water

For 10 oz (300 g) of sourdough starter

1½ cups (150 g) bread flour

⅔ cup (150 ml) water,

room temperature

If you're looking for a simple method for homemade bread, here's your recipe.
You'll need a conventional oven, flour, salt, water, and a little patience.
Here we explain how to make your own sourdough starter for a more interesting taste
than fermentation with industrial yeast provides.
Feel free to add spices, dried fruits, or nuts to the dough.

Step One

Two days ahead, make the sourdough starter: in a mixing bowl, combine 1 cup (100 g) flour
with ½ cup (100 ml) water. Cover the mixture with a damp cloth. Every three hours, stir the
mixture to activate the fermentation and cover again. This should be done about five times.
Refrigerate overnight.

The next day, add ½ cup (50 g) flour and ¼ cup (50 ml) water. Again, stir every three hours
and cover with a damp cloth. Repeat the operation altogether about five times. Refrigerate
a second night.

The sourdough starter is now ready.

For the bread recipe, you'll only need ½ lb (200 g) of the starter. With the remaining starter,
you can repeat the process as many times as you wish, adding ½ cup (50 g) flour and ¼ cup
(50 ml) water each time.

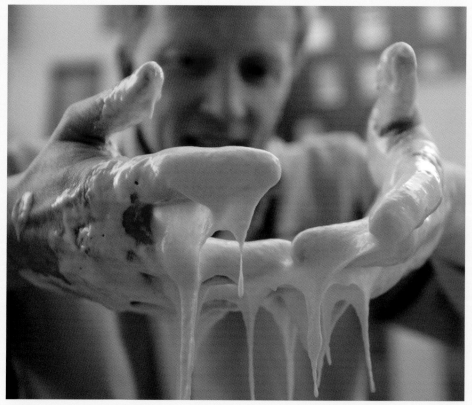

Step Two
Place the flour in a bowl or on a clean work surface and make two small wells in the flour. Add the yeast to one and the salt to the other, taking care that the salt and the yeast don't come into direct contact.

Mix in the sourdough starter.
Pour in the water, which should be at room temperature, and knead well.

Stretch out the dough, pulling it toward you, to increase elasticity. Fold the part of the dough that you've pulled over the remaining part to strengthen its structure and incorporate air into it.

Give the dough a quarter turn and repeat the process. For this part of the procedure to be effective, you should spend 15 to 20 minutes pulling and folding.

Cover the dough with a damp cloth and leave for 1 hour at room temperature.

Step Three

Using a small, thin knife, divide the dough into five loaves weighing ¾ lb (360 g) each.

With the palm of your hand, flatten the dough to form a disc. Don't press too hard.

Take hold of a side of the disc and fold over one-third of the dough. Press it down over the rest of the dough, applying light pressure with the palms of your hands.

Take the folded side, and repeat the operation of folding and pressing.

Just a small part of the dough will remain unfolded. Turn this inward to form the final shape of the bread. Cover and let stand for 1 ½ hours.

Step Four

Place some water in an ovenproof bowl at the bottom of the oven.

Preheat the oven to 250° F (120° C) and place a baking tray in the oven.
Cover another baking tray with waxed paper and place the loaf on this.
Make incisions on the top of the loaf, letting the blade of the knife penetrate to just below the surface. Two incisions measuring 2 ½ inches (5 cm) are enough, because the dough is going to rise.

Slide the bread onto the hot tray to create the effect of a hearth oven.
After 10 minutes' baking, remove the bowl of water.
Continue baking for 15 minutes. The crust should be nicely browned.

Turn the bread onto a wire rack and leave to cool for at least 1 hour, in a dry, well-aired place.

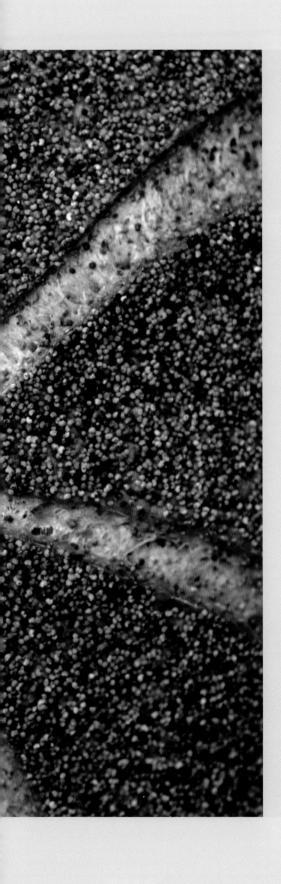

Bread
and
Your Health

Bread is at the very core of Western civilization, of its history, of its beliefs, and even of its wars. Reams of paper have been covered on the subject of bread. For centuries, bread was synonymous with the food of the masses, but in the 1970s it was decried as being a major cause of modern obesity. Since then, of course, nutritionists have vigorously rejected this idea, but it is still important to remind everyone of the benefits of bread, or rather, of bread made by bakers using traditional methods. If we know how different types of bread contribute to our health, we will improve our understanding of how to eat them.

A food to supplement

We all know that man cannot live by bread alone, since it does not contain all the nutriments we need. Although bread contains proteins, minerals (chlorine, sodium, magnesium, potassium, and iron), and vitamins (B1, B2, PP, and E), there are not enough of these for a well-balanced diet. The mineral content is too low to ensure good health and certain vitamins, such as A and C, are lacking. In addition to bread, we need to complete our intake with foods such as fruit, vegetables, and meat.

Reduce your cravings effectively with bread

There are many good reasons to eat bread. Firstly, when it is being digested, it fills the stomach, reducing your craving for other foods. Unlike foods high in simple sugars, it gradually provides energy to the body, thereby reducing your sensation of hunger for a longer period. What's more, it's rich in vegetable protein, far less harmful than animal protein. This reduces the risk of cardiovascular problems. Today's eating habits mean we eat too much fat and sugar, known to contribute to obesity. Because it is low in fats and simple carbohydrates, eating bread helps us balance our meals.

Each type of bread has specific nutritional qualities

Breads vary in their nutritional value. The various cereals in different types of bread mean that each one can provide something specific. Bran bread, for example, is high in fiber, so it helps the digestive process. Spelt contains four times as much magnesium as wheat. Buckwheat is known to be a good source of protein. Of course it's wholewheat bread that provides the widest variety of nutriments. The starter used in sourdough bread helps the body assimilate the minerals and vitamins it contains. Because numerous additives are allowed to be used in bread, it's preferable to buy your bread from a baker you can depend on to maintain bread-making traditions. Bread is an essential part of the food you need; it shouldn't be forgotten when you're planning your balanced meals.

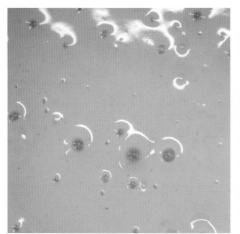

A food to enjoy

Now, more than ever, with a return to a healthy diet comprising simple, good-quality foods, bread is once again taking its place on our tables. There's hardly anyone who doesn't enjoy good bread, and one of its main advantages—not to be forgotten—is the pleasure it gives. Today, I try to produce bread that is healthy for everyone. I use starters rather than yeast, keep salt to a minimum, and don't add preservatives. Please try all these breads made from different flours and grains: they're all good for you, so you can eat them all with a *bon appétit*!

Using Bread
as a Plate

FIG BRUSCHETTA
WITH CHICKEN LIVERS AND ORANGES

Serves 4
Preparation time: 15 minutes
Cooking time: 5 minutes

Ingredients
7 oz (200 g) chicken livers
4 oranges
1 x 10 oz (300 g) fig bread, sliced
¼ cup (50 g) unsalted butter
2 tablespoons (30 ml) Grand Marnier
8 celery leaves, cut in four,
for decoration
Salt and pepper to taste

Dry the chicken livers on paper towel and separate the lobes.

Peel three oranges and separate them into segments. Set aside.

Toast 8 slices of fig bread.

Heat a frying pan and melt the butter. Quickly brown the chicken livers in the sizzling butter. Season with salt and pepper. Deglaze the pan with the Grand Marnier and the juice of the remaining orange.

Alternate the orange segments and the chicken livers on the fig bread. Decorate with the celery leaves, and serve immediately.

Baker's tip
To serve these as appetizers with drinks, you can cut the slices of bread into small pieces.

OLIVE BREAD BOWLS WITH THREE-MEAT RAGOUT

Serves 4
Preparation time: 20 minutes
Cooking time: 40 minutes

Ingredients

4 shallots
3 lb (1.5 kg) tomatoes
⅔ cup (150 ml) olive oil
½ lb (250 g) minced lamb
½ lb (250 g) minced beef
½ lb (250 g) minced pork
4 x ½ lb (250 g) olive loaves
½ lb (250 g) Italian soft mozzarella
1 bunch of basil to garnish
Salt and pepper to taste

Peel and chop the shallots.
Pour boiling water over the tomatoes, remove them after 30 seconds, and peel them.
Dice into small cubes.

Heat the olive oil to a high temperature in a frying pan. Sauté the chopped shallots, then add the minced meats. Season with salt and pepper. As soon as the meat starts to brown, add the cubed tomatoes, stir, and leave to simmer for 30 minutes.

While the meat mixture is cooking, cut the top off each loaf and remove the soft inner part of each one to form a bowl shape.

Preheat the oven to 350° F (180° C). Place the loaves on a baking tray.
Cut the mozzarella into 12 slices.

As soon as the ragout is ready, spoon it into the bread bowls, and top each one with three slices of mozzarella.

Place in the oven for 5 minutes until the cheese melts.

Decorate with basil leaves, and serve immediately.

Wine suggestion
Accompany this dish with a full-bodied, hearty red wine.

OPEN SANDWICHES WITH FINELY SLICED MUSHROOMS, RADISH SPROUTS, AND FINE STRIPS OF CURED HAM

Serves 4
Preparation time: 20 minutes
Cooking time: 20 minutes

Ingredients

1 lb (400 g) button mushrooms
½ lb (200 g) onions
¼ cup (50 ml) olive oil
1 cup (250 ml) red wine
1 ½ lb (250 g) fig loaf, sliced
1 ½ oz (40 g) radish sprouts
(available in organic stores)
¼ lb (140 g) Jabugo or other cured ham
Salt and pepper to taste

Trim the mushroom stalks and rinse the mushrooms. Chop them finely.

Peel the onions and chop them finely.

Heat the olive oil in a frying pan and sauté the chopped onion.
Add the mushrooms. When they are cooked, deglaze with the red wine.
Season with salt and pepper.

Remove from heat as soon as the texture becomes fairly compact.
Toast 8 slices of fig loaf.

Spread the mushroom mixture thinly on each slice of toast. Arrange the radish sprouts and wafer slices of ham attractively over the mushrooms.

Baker's tip
When chanterelles and cèpes are in season, use these instead of button mushrooms. If you don't have radish sprouts, you can use small arugula leaves.

25

SUN-DRIED TOMATO BRUSCHETTA WITH TOMATO-MOZZARELLA SKEWERS

Serves 4

Preparation time: 25 minutes

Ingredients

6 tomatoes, fresh off the vine

1 x ½ lb (250 g) sun-dried tomato bread

1 lb (500 g) Italian soft mozzarella

Salt and pepper to taste

For the pesto

2 oz (50 g) fresh mint

1 oz (25 g) toasted pine nuts

¾ cup (200 ml) olive oil

2 garlic cloves, chopped

Salt and pepper to taste

Blend the pesto Ingredients well (mint, pine nuts, olive oil, and garlic). Season with salt and pepper.

Pour boiling water over the tomatoes, remove them after 30 seconds, and peel them. Cut into quarters and seed them. Mix in a little of the mint pesto.

Cut the mozzarella cheese into 24 slices.

On each skewer, alternate the tomato quarters and mozzarella slices, using 3 of each.

Spread the mint pesto over the bread slices and stick a tomato–mozzarella skewer into each one.

Baker's tip

You can use olive bread instead of sun-dried tomato bread.

SEAWEED BREAD TAPAS WITH SMOKED SALMON, AVOCADO, AND CARAMELIZED FENNEL

Serves 4
Preparation time: 20 minutes
Cooking time: 10 minutes

Ingredients

4 x 2 ½ oz (80 g) seaweed bread rolls
2 avocados
4 slices smoked salmon
4 mini fennel bulbs
2 tablespoons (30 ml) olive oil
Salt and pepper to taste

Cut the rolls in half and toast them until they turn a golden color.

Peel the avocados, and use a vegetable peeler to cut the flesh into thin wafers. Cut the smoked salmon slices into two.

Roll each half-slice together with 2 slivers of avocado.

Cut the fennel bulbs in half lengthways.

Heat a frying pan, pour in the olive oil, and gently fry the fennel for about 10 minutes, or until it turns a golden color. Season with salt and pepper.

Place an avocado-salmon roll, together with half a sautéed fennel bulb, on each slice of toast, and serve immediately.

Baker's tip

If you can't find seaweed bread, wrap the rolls in seaweed for sushi from a Japanese food store.

RED ONION FOUGASSE

Serves 4
Preparation time: 10 minutes
Cooking time: 20 minutes

Ingredients

⅔ cup (150 ml) olive oil
2 handfuls of pine nuts
4 red onions
1 lb (500 g) fougasse dough, flavored
with herbes de Provence (thyme,
rosemary, oregano, etc.), obtained
from your baker, or use the bread
recipe given below
1 oz (25 g) anchovies, canned in oil
Freshly ground pepper to taste

Preheat the oven to 450° F (240° C).

Heat 2 tablespoons (30 ml) olive oil in a frying pan and gently fry the pine nuts.
Peel the onions, cut them in half, and slice them finely.

Cover a pastry board with waxed paper and roll out the fougasse dough to a thickness of just under ½ inch (1 cm).

Finely chop the anchovies. Put them in a bowl and mix together with the olive oil, the onions, and the pine nuts.

Spread this mixture over the dough and season with freshly ground pepper.

Bake for about 10–15 minutes, until the dough turns golden brown.

Serve hot.

Baker's tip

You can make the fougasse dough yourself, using 2 ½ cups (250 g) flour, ½ cup (125 ml) olive oil, 1 teaspoon salt, 5 g (¼ oz) fresh yeast, 4 tablespoons herbes de Provence, and ¾ teaspoon sugar. Put all the ingredients into the bowl of a food processor together with 1 cup (250 ml) water. Knead for 10 minutes at low speed.
Roll out the dough and leave to rise at room temperature for 1 hour.

BAGUETTE PIZZA

Serves 4
Preparation time: 10 minutes
Cooking time: 15 minutes

Ingredients

2 baguettes
4 tablespoons (60 ml) olive oil
1 lb (500 g) cherry tomatoes
½ lb (250 g) sun-dried tomatoes
4 shallots
½ lb (250 g) Italian soft mozzarella
2 handfuls of unsalted pistachio nuts, shelled
Salt and pepper to taste

Preheat the oven to 400° F (210° C).

Cut the baguettes in half lengthways. Drizzle olive oil over each half.

Toast the baguettes in the oven for 5 minutes. Remove and leave the oven on.

Blend the cherry tomatoes and the dried tomatoes together thoroughly to make a paste. Season with salt and pepper.

Finely slice the shallots and cut the mozzarella into thin slices of about ¼ inch (0.5 cm).

Spread the tomato paste over the baguettes. Arrange the mozzarella slices over it, and spoon the sliced shallots over the mozzarella. Sprinkle with the pistachios. Bake for 7 minutes or until the cheese has melted.

Baker's tip
In the south of France, these baguette pizzas are called *mandolines*.

WALNUT BREAD QUICHE
WITH TURNIPS AND CABBAGE

Serves 8
Preparation time: 20 minutes
Cooking time: 45 minutes

Ingredients

5 eggs
1 ½ cups (350 ml) whole milk
1 ½ cups (350 ml) crème fraîche or
heavy cream
2 lb (1 kg) walnut bread dough
(order from your baker, or make
it yourself, modifying
the recipe on page 10 as below)
1 lb (500 g) turnips
1 small white or Chinese cabbage
Salt and pepper to taste

↻ A day ahead

Prepare the quiche mixture: in a bowl, mix the eggs, milk, and crème fraîche together. Season with salt and pepper. Refrigerate overnight.

✻ Prepare the filling

Preheat the oven to 350° F (180° C).

Roll the walnut bread dough to fit a 10 inch (26 cm) square pan. Prick the dough lightly and regularly with a fork. Line the dough with aluminum foil and weigh it down with pulses (dried beans or lentils, for example) to prevent it from rising. Bake for 20 minutes.

Peel the turnips and wash the cabbage.
Finely slice the vegetables.

When the pastry is baked, remove the pan from the oven, leaving the oven on. Arrange the sliced vegetables in the pastry shell, alternating cabbage and turnip layers. Pour the quiche mixture over. Bake for 25 minutes until golden brown.

Baker's tip

If you make the dough yourself, you can halve the proportions given on page 10 and add 3 oz (100 g) walnuts.

MINI RUSTIC BREAD TARTLETS WITH SAUTÉED MUSHROOMS

Serves 4
Preparation time: 15 minutes
Cooking time: 10 minutes

Ingredients

8 slices of rustic bread (sourdough)
½ lb (250 g) button mushrooms
3 tablespoons (45 ml) olive oil
1 bunch chives, snipped
Salt and pepper to taste

Preheat the oven to 350°C (180°F).

Use a tartlet mold to cut out round shapes from the rustic bread.

Toast the bread slices in the oven for 7 minutes.

Trim the mushroom stems and wash the mushrooms.

Cut them into very fine slices (less than ¼ inch / 0.5 cm thick).

Heat the olive oil in a frying pan and sauté the mushrooms. Season with salt and pepper.

Arrange the mushrooms attractively over the round slices of bread. Sprinkle with chives.

Baker's tip

For an even tastier treat, replace the button mushrooms with cèpes.

TURMERIC BREAD BOWL WITH ROASTED VEGETABLE SALAD

Serves 4
Preparation time: 15 minutes
Cooking time: 30 minutes

Ingredients

For the salad

1 ¼ lb (600 g) broccoli florets
1 ¼ lb (600 g) eggplants
4 tablespoons (60 ml) olive oil
1 x 1 lb (500 g) turmeric and hazelnut bread
1 bunch basil
Coarse salt
Salt and freshly ground pepper to taste

For the sauce

¾ cup (200 ml) coconut milk
Juice and zest of ½ lime
1 teaspoon (5 ml) soy sauce

Preheat the oven to 425° F (210° C).

Cut the broccoli into small florets, drizzle with olive oil, and season with salt and pepper. Broil in the oven for 15 minutes.

Cut each eggplant lengthways into 12 slices. Drizzle with olive oil, and season with coarse salt and ground pepper. Broil in the oven for 15 minutes at the same temperature.

Form a salad bowl from the bread by cutting off the top and removing the soft inner part. Mix the coconut milk, the grated lime zest, the lime juice, and the soy sauce. Refrigerate.

Place the broiled vegetables in the "bread bowl" and add whole basil leaves. Pour the dressing over and eat immediately, using your fingers to help yourselves from the bread bowl.

Baker's tip

If you can't find turmeric bread, you can use walnut bread and add 1 scant teaspoon turmeric to the sauce.

LARGE RUSTIC BREAD SALAD BOWL WITH HERITAGE VEGETABLES

Serves 8
Preparation time: 15 minutes
Cooking time: 20 minutes

Ingredients

1 lb (500 g) red onions
1 lb (500 g) sweet potatoes
1 lb (500 g) parsnips
1 lb (500 g) Jerusalem artichokes
¾ cup (200 ml) olive oil
1 x 3 ½ lb (1.8 kg) loaf of
rustic bread (sourdough)
1 lemon
1 bunch of chervil
Salt and pepper to taste

Preheat the oven to 425° F (210° C).

Peel the onions and cut them into 6.
Peel the other vegetables, and cut them into strips 2 to 3 inches (5 to 7 cm) long.
Mix the olive oil into the cut vegetables and onions. Season with salt and pepper.

Broil the vegetables in an oven-proof dish for 20 minutes, turning them regularly so that they are browned on all sides.

Cut off the top of the bread and empty out the soft part to create a salad bowl. Keep the top to use as a decorative lid.

Let the broiled vegetables cool off slightly, and spoon them into the bread bowl. Pour the lemon juice over them and sprinkle with chervil leaves.

Put the lid on the top and serve.

Baker's tip
You can eat the salad bowl, which will absorb the taste of the vegetables.

OPEN SANDWICHES WITH LEMON-FLAVORED PERSIMMONS AND FENNEL

Serves 4
Preparation time: 15 minutes

Ingredients

1 x ½ lb (250 g) olive bread
2 persimmons
1 fennel bulb
2 zucchini
2 tablespoons (30 ml) olive oil
Juice of ½ lemon
Salt and pepper to taste

Cut the olive bread in 4 slices lengthways.

Cut the persimmons in 6 pieces.

Wash the fennel and the zucchini. Using a mandolin vegetable slicer or peeler, cut the vegetables very finely. Place them in a mixing bowl.

Pour the olive oil and lemon juice over the vegetables.
Season with salt and pepper.

Toast the bread and arrange the fruit and vegetables over the slices.

Wine suggestion

Serve with an aromatic white wine, such as a Riesling.

Using Bread as an Ingredient

MILDLY SPICED MINCED LAMB
IN A BREAD POCKET

Serves 4
Preparation time: 20 minutes
Resting time: 20 minutes
Cooking time: 25 minutes

Ingredients

2 onions
⅓ cup (75 ml) olive oil
1 lb (500 g) minced lamb
2 tablespoons ground cinnamon
2 lb (1 kg) bread dough (ask your baker
or use the recipe on page 10)
Salt and pepper to taste

Peel the onions and cut them into fine rings.
Heat the oil in a pan and brown the onions.

Add the minced lamb and the cinnamon, and season with salt and pepper.
Cook over a medium heat until the meat is browned and cooked through.

Roll out the bread dough to a thickness of about ¼ inch (0.5 cm).

Using a pastry cutter or the rim of a cup, cut out 4 inch (10 cm) diameter circles of dough.
Place 1 spoonful of meat mixture in the center of each circle and fold up three sides
of the circle to form a triangle, leaving a hole in the center. Pinch the sides of the
dough together.

Preheat the oven to 400° F (200° C).

Cover a baking pan with waxed paper and place the triangles there for 20 minutes
at room temperature to rest.

Bake the meat triangles for 20 minutes until the pastry is golden brown.

Baker's tip
As an alternative, add pine nuts and raisins to the meat mixture.

TUNA AND SHALLOT TARTAR ON SEAWEED BREAD

Serves 4

Preparation time: 10 minutes

Ingredients

1 lb (500 g) ultra-fresh tuna
1 shallot
3 oz (100 g) radishes
Zest and juice of 1 unwaxed lime
½ cup (100 ml) olive oil
1 x ½ lb (250 g) loaf of rye bread with seaweed

Finely dice the tuna fish.

Cut the shallot and radishes into thin slices.

Mix the lime zest, the sliced shallot, and ¼ cup (50 ml) olive oil into the diced tuna. Cut the bread into small cubes and mix it with the radish slices, the juice of half the lime, and the rest of the olive oil.

Take a 4 inch (10 cm) cookie cutter and fill up halfway with the bread mixture. Cover with the tuna mixture. Don't pack it in too firmly. Unmold on to a serving plate and repeat with the remaining mixture to make 4 servings.

Baker's tip

If you don't have seaweed bread, you can add chopped nori (Japanese seaweed). Even simpler, use classic rye bread.

CHICKEN WITH PRUNE STUFFING

Serves 4
Preparation time: 25 minutes
Cooking time: 55 minutes

Ingredients

3 oz (100 g) chicken livers
2 tablespoons (30 g) unsalted butter
1 oz (25 g) pitted prunes
1 oz (25 g) hazelnuts
½ baguette, best if slightly stale
1 egg, beaten
¼ cup (50 ml) milk
1 free-range chicken
3 tablespoons (45 ml) olive oil
Salt and pepper to taste

Preheat the oven to 425° F (210° C).

Pat the chicken livers dry using a paper towel.

Melt the butter in a frying pan and sear the chicken livers for three minutes. Set aside. Chop the prunes, the hazelnuts, and the dry bread. Incorporate the egg and the milk. Pull the chicken livers apart without separating the lobes and add to the stuffing. Season with salt and pepper.

Fill the chicken cavity with the stuffing and truss the bird. Baste it with olive oil.

Lay it breast side down and cook for 25 minutes, then turn it and continue cooking for 30 minutes until the chicken is cooked through.

Wine suggestion

Serve with a fine, aromatic wine such as a light-bodied Burgundy red.

CHERRY TOMATO GAZPACHO AND RUSTIC BREAD

Serves 4
Preparation time: 15 minutes
Cooking time: 15 minutes

Ingredients

2 lb (1 kg) cherry tomatoes
4 tablespoons (60 ml) olive oil
1 red bell pepper
4 x ½ lb (250 g) small round rustic
loaves (sourdough)
Summer savory or thyme flowers
Salt and pepper to taste

Preheat the oven to 250° F (120° C).

Blend the cherry tomatoes with the olive oil.
Remove the seeds from the bell pepper and cut it into pieces. Blend them with the tomatoes and the oil.

Cut off the tops of the loaves and empty them out, setting aside 6 oz (180 g) of the soft inner part, to form soup bowls. Drizzle a little olive oil over them and bake in the oven for 15 minutes. Remove from the oven and leave to cool.
Add the reserved soft part of the bread to the tomato and pepper mixture, and blend the ingredients together. Season with salt and pepper.

When the bread bowls have cooled down, pour in the gazpacho and scatter with the summer savory or thyme flowers.

Baker's tip

In this recipe, the acidity of the sourdough rustic bread replaces the sherry vinegar usually used. This is why it's essential to use a bread with natural leavening.

SEAWEED MILLE-FEUILLE
WITH BEETS AND SCALLOPS

Serves 4
Preparation time: 20 minutes
Cooking time: 5 minutes

Ingredients

1 x ½ lb (250 g) seaweed loaf
½ lb (250 g) cooked beets
1 ⅔ cups (400 ml) whipping cream
8 scallops
2 tablespoons (30 ml) olive oil
Salt and pepper to taste

Cut the bread into thin slices about ¼ inch (0.5 cm) thick. Toast them.

Blend the beets with the whipping cream until the mixture forms a creamy texture.

Shuck the scallops, open them, and place the roe and white flesh in a bowl of cold water for a few minutes. Heat the olive oil in a pan and sear the scallops, 2 to 3 minutes on each side. Season with salt and pepper.

Place a slice of toast on each plate, and put a spoonful of beet mousse on the toast. Place a second slice of toast on the mousse, and on this put 2 scallops. Serve immediately.

Baker's tip
These mille-feuilles taste good with a crisp green salad.

MEATBALLS
WITH CHESTNUT BREAD

Serves 4
Preparation time: 20 minutes
Cooking time: 10 minutes

Ingredients

1 shallot
5 oz (150 g) chestnut bread
1 lb (500 g) minced beef
1 egg, beaten
½ cup (100 g) melted butter
or grapeseed oil

For the sauce

⅔ cup (150 g) heavy cream
or crème fraîche
1 ½ tablespoons (25 ml)
balsamic vinegar

Peel and finely slice the shallot.

Cut the bread into small cubes.

In a bowl, mix together the meat, the bread cubes, the shallot, and the egg. Heat the melted butter or the oil in a frying pan. (The fat should be no more than ¼ inch / 0.5 cm deep at the bottom of the pan.)

With wet hands, shape the meat mixture into small balls, and fry over a medium heat.

Mix the crème fraîche and balsamic vinegar together, and serve the sauce with the meatballs.

Baker's tip

If you don't have chestnut bread, use 3 oz (100 g) of sourdough bread and add 1 oz (30 g) ready-to-use peeled chestnuts.

ROASTED VEGETABLE POCKETS

Serves 4
Preparation time: 30 minutes
Cooking time: 1 hour

Ingredients

2 red bell peppers
2 parsnips
1 sweet potato
3 zucchini
2 tablespoons (30 ml) olive oil
1 lb (500 g) buckwheat bread dough (ask
your baker, or prepare at home)
Salt and pepper to taste

Preheat the oven to 400° F (210° C).

Wash the bell peppers, line a baking tray with waxed paper, and broil them for 20 minutes.

Peel them and remove the pips. Leave whole if possible.
Peel the parsnips and the sweet potato. Wash the zucchini. Cut these vegetables into ½ inch (1 cm) wide strips. Drizzle the olive oil over the strips and season with salt and pepper.

Spread the vegetables (except the bell peppers) over a baking tray and broil for 15 minutes in the oven.

Roll the dough out to a rectangle just under ½ inch (1 cm) thick. Arrange the broiled vegetables and the bell peppers in a line along the middle third of the rectangle.
Fold up the sides of the dough as if making a turnover and seal at each end.

Bake for 25 minutes at the same temperature until risen and browned.

Slice and serve.

Baker's tip
You might want to choose other vegetables like carrots, eggplant, turnips, etc.

TOAST TAPENADE

Serves 4
Preparation time: 15 minutes

Ingredients

2 slices of sourdough bread
2 oz (50 g) pecan nuts
2 oz (50 g) hazelnuts
2 oz (50 g) walnuts
4 tablespoons (60 ml) olive oil
3 tablespoons (45 ml) water
3 oz (100 g) liquid sourdough starter
(see recipe page 10)
Salt and pepper to taste

Toast the sourdough bread.

Grind the pecans, hazelnuts, walnuts, and sourdough bread toast together.
Add the olive oil and the water. Blend again until the mixture becomes foamy.

Stir in the liquid leavening just before serving.

Serve with a hard or blue cheese and cut fruit such as grapes.

Baker's tip

If you don't have any sourdough starter, you can use 1 tablespoon plus 1 teaspoon (20 ml) sherry vinegar.

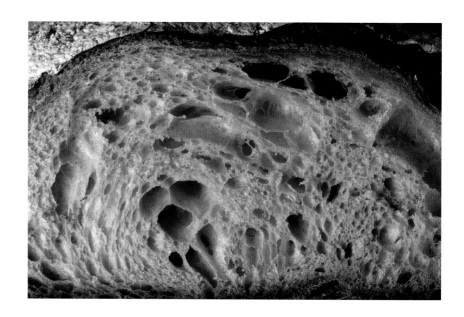

SALAD OF TUNA *À L'UNILATÉRALE* WITH POPPY SEED BREAD

Serves 4
Preparation time: 20 minutes
Cooking time: 7 minutes

Ingredients
4 slices poppy seed bread
2 fennel bulbs
3 tablespoons (45 ml) olive oil
4 tuna fillets
Salt and pepper to taste

For the pesto
2 oz (50 g) leek sprouts
(available in organic food stores)
1 oz (25 g) unsalted, shelled pistachios
7 oz (200 g) wakame seaweed
3 tablespoons (50 ml) olive oil
3 tablespoons (50 ml) water

Prepare the pesto: blend the leek sprouts, the pistachios, the seaweed, the oil, and the water together.

Toast the bread and cut it into large croutons.

Wash the fennel, then slice it finely. Lightly fry it in the olive oil. Season with salt and pepper.

Dry the tuna fillets using paper towel. Sear them in a frying pan for 2 minutes on one side only (i.e., *à l'unilatérale*).

Cut each fillet into 3 pieces.

On each plate, arrange the tuna, the croutons, and the fennel. Drizzle the seaweed pesto over the salad, and serve immediately.

Baker's tip
If you can't find leek sprouts, shred a small leek finely.

SARDINE-STUFFED BAGUETTE

Serves 4
Preparation time: 20 minutes
Resting time: 1 hour
Cooking time: 25 minutes

Ingredients
1 shallot
4 fresh sardines
1 ¾ lb (800 g) bread dough (ask your baker, or prepare at home)
Salt and pepper to taste
Peel and slice the shallot finely.

Gut the sardines and wash them. Fillet each fish.

Divide the dough into 4 equal pieces. Roll each piece into an oval just under ½ inch (1 cm) thick. Place a sardine fillet in the middle of each oval and sprinkle with the shredded shallot. Season with salt and pepper and place another sardine fillet on top.

Wrap the dough around the filling so that it is a little shorter than a baguette.

Leave to rest for 1 hour at room temperature.

Preheat the oven to 425° F (210° C).

Make incisions in the upper side of the dough and bake on a baking tray for 25 minutes until golden brown and risen.

What inspired this recipe
This idea came from a sandwich that was popular with French factory workers in the early twentieth century.

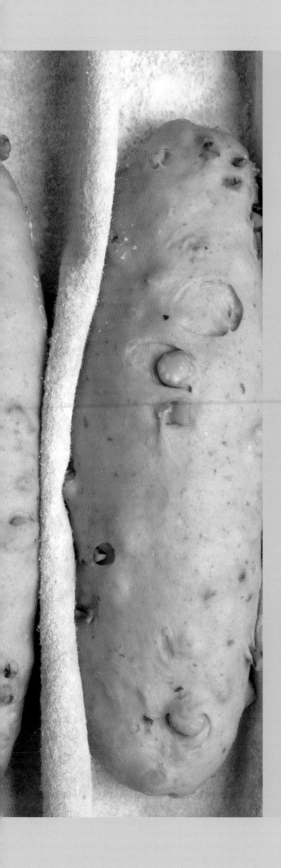

Using Bread
as a Seasoning

BRAISED SWEET POTATO, TOFU, AND CROUTON SALAD

Serves 4
Preparation time: 20 minutes
Cooking time: 30 minutes

Ingredients
For the salad

4 slices turmeric bread
½ lb (250 g) tofu
1 lb (500 g) sweet potatoes
3 tablespoons (45 ml) olive oil
1 ½ tablespoons (25 ml)
balsamic vinegar
2 teaspoons coarse salt
Pepper to taste

For the walnut salad dressing

⅓ cup (70 ml)
olive oil
2 tablespoons (15 g) finely
chopped walnuts
2 teaspoons (10 ml) balsamic vinegar
Salt and pepper to taste

Preheat the oven to 200° F (100° C). Cut the slices of turmeric bread into cubes and let them dry out in the oven for 10 minutes. Set aside. Increase the oven temperature to 425° F (210° C).

Peel the sweet potatoes. Cut them into cubes just under 1 inch by 1 inch (2 x 2 cm). Cut the tofu into cubes the same size.

In a large mixing bowl, combine the olive oil, the balsamic vinegar, the salt, and the pepper. Add the tofu and sweet potato cubes, mix to coat the cubes, then place them on a baking tray, and broil for 20 minutes.

Combine the oil, walnuts, vinegar, salt, and pepper to make the salad dressing.

Place the tofu and the sweet potato in 4 bowls and add the croutons. Spoon the dressing over the salad.

Baker's tip
If you don't have turmeric bread, use walnut bread and add 1 ¾ teaspoons ground turmeric to the dressing.

FRIED SHRIMP WITH
ORANGE-FLAVORED BREADCRUMBS

Serves 4
Preparation time: 20 minutes
Cooking time: 10 minutes

Ingredients

5 oz (150 g) orange-flavored bread
1 lb (500 g) raw shrimp
3 tablespoons (50 ml) olive oil
Salt and pepper to taste

Slice and toast the bread. Process the toast in a food processor to make fine breadcrumbs.

Rinse the shrimps and peel off the shell, keeping the head and the tail.

Heat the olive oil to a high temperature in a frying pan.

Sauté the shrimps rapidly and add the breadcrumbs. Season with salt and pepper.

Serve immediately.

Baker's tip
If you can't find orange-flavored bread, add the grated zest of an orange to the breadcrumbs.

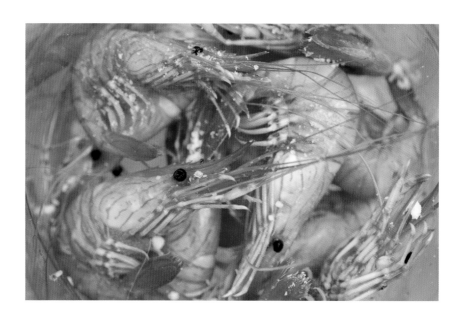

EGGPLANT PÂTÉ
AND BAGUETTE CHIPS

Serves 4
Preparation time: 20 minutes
Cooking time: 30 minutes

Ingredients
4 eggplants
2 red onions
1 baguette
1 ½ tablespoons (25 ml) olive oil
1 bunch of flat-leafed parsley
Fleur de sel (sea salt from Brittany
or the Camargue) to taste
Pepper to taste

Preheat the oven to 350° F (180° C).

Wash the eggplants. Prick them with a knife and broil them in the oven for 20–25 minutes, until very soft.

Peel the onions and slice them into fine rings.

Cut the baguette into 12 slices ½ inch (1 cm) thick.

Place the onion rings on the bread slices and drizzle a few drops of olive oil over them.

Grill them in the oven until they turn golden.

Remove the ends of the eggplants and peel them.

Make three crosswise slits in the middle of each eggplant and insert the onion and baguette chips.

 Season with olive oil, fleur de sel, pepper, and a few leaves of flat-leafed parsley.

Baker's tip
You can use a piece of slightly stale baguette to enhance the contrast between the textures of the tender eggplant and the crisp chips.

SCALLOPS TOPPED WITH TOASTED BREADCRUMBS

Serves 4
Preparation time: 20 minutes
Cooking time: 8 minutes

Ingredients

12 scallops
3 oz (100 g) multigrain bread
½ cup (100 g) salted butter, softened
3 tablespoons (45 ml) olive oil
Salt and pepper to taste

Shuck the scallops, open them, and place the roe and white flesh in a bowl of cold water for a few minutes. Clean and dry the empty shells.

Slice and toast the bread. Grind it in the food processor. Combine the breadcrumbs and the softened butter.

Preheat the oven grill.

Heat the olive oil and sear the scallops for 2 minutes on one side only.

Put a scallop into a half shell, seared side downwards.

Top each scallop with a layer of butter-breadcrumb mixture, less than a ¼ inch (0.5 cm) thick.

Bake on a tray directly under the grill for 3 minutes and serve immediately.

Wine suggestion

Serve with a top-quality Chablis.

BLACK PUDDING AND CARAMELIZED APPLES IN A GINGERBREAD CRUST

Serves 4
Preparation time: 20 minutes
Cooking time: 30 minutes

Ingredients
½ lb (250 g) apples,
preferably Granny Smith
½ cup (100 g) granulated sugar
1 lb (500 g) blood sausage
(a.k.a. black pudding)
5 oz (150 g) gingerbread

Peel and core the apples. Dice them into 1 inch (2.5 cm) cubes.

Pour the sugar into a saucepan. Cook over a low heat, stirring constantly, until it melts and turns golden brown. Add the apple cubes and leave them to simmer gently for 15 minutes, until the texture reaches that of a thick applesauce.

Preheat the oven to 350° F (180° C).

Cut the blood sausage in half lengthways.

Cut the gingerbread into thin slices.

Line a tart dish with waxed paper and place the blood sausage on it. Cover this with a ½ inch (1 cm) layer of applesauce, and then with the gingerbread slices.

Bake for 5 minutes.

Cut into 4 parts and serve immediately.

Baker's tip
If you like spices, add cinnamon when preparing the applesauce.

AVOCADO SOUP
WITH TOASTED MULTIGRAIN BREAD

Serves 6
Preparation time: 20 minutes
Cooking time: 15 minutes

Ingredients

2 slices of multigrain bread
1 bunch radishes
2 tablespoons (30 ml) olive oil
1 handful of pine nuts
4 avocados
Juice of 1 lemon
2/3 cup (150 ml) cold water
Salt and pepper to taste

Preheat the oven to 200° F (100° C). Dice the multigrain bread. Let the bread cubes dry out in the oven for 10 minutes to make croutons. Set aside.

Wash the radishes and remove most of the stalks. Cut into quarters.

Heat the olive oil and lightly sauté the pine nuts.

Peel the avocados. Blend the pulp with the lemon juice and the cold water. Season with salt and pepper.

Spoon the avocado soup into 4 bowls. Add the croutons, the radishes, and the pine nuts.

Baker's tip

Choose very ripe avocados, preferably of the Hass variety, which has dark and rough skin.

KAYSER SALAD

Serves 4
Preparation time: 30 minutes
Marinate for 30 minutes
Cooking time: 45 minutes

Ingredients

2 whole chicken breasts or 4 halves
5 tablespoons (75 ml) olive oil
½ teaspoon ground piment d'Espelette
(chili pepper from the Basque region)
4 slices of cocoa bread
1 large head Romaine lettuce
2 handfuls pecan nuts

For the sauce

1 eggplant
3 oz (100 g) grated Parmesan cheese
3 tablespoons (60 ml) crème fraîche or
heavy cream
Salt to taste

Preheat the oven to 425° F (210° C).

If using whole chicken breasts, cut them into halves. Marinade them in the fridge for 30 minutes in 3 tablespoons (45 ml) of the olive oil mixed with the piment d'Espelette.

Wash the eggplant and broil it on a baking tray for 25 minutes. Turn the temperature down to 200° F (100° C). Peel the eggplant. Blend the flesh with the Parmesan cheese and the cream. Set aside.

Cut the cocoa bread into cubes and dry them out in the oven for 10 minutes. Set aside. Wash and dry the lettuce.

Heat the remaining 2 tablespoons (30 ml) of olive oil and brown the pecan nuts. In another frying pan, at moderate temperature, grill the chicken pieces. Cut each one into three.

Put the lettuce leaves into a salad bowl. Add the chicken, the pecan nuts, and the croutons. Season with the eggplant sauce.

Baker's tip

If you don't have cocoa bread, sprinkle a sourdough loaf with a little cocoa powder.

GRILLED GOAT CHEESE
WITH WHOLEWHEAT BREADSTICKS

Serves 4
Preparation time: 10 minutes
Cooking time: 10 minutes

Ingredients

2 slices of wholewheat bread
1 bunch of rosemary
4 small, creamy goat cheeses

Toast the bread. Cut the slices into sticks ¼ inch (0.5 cm) wide. Set aside.

Preheat the oven to 350° F (180° C).

Separate the sprigs of rosemary.

Insert the breadsticks and the rosemary sprigs around the goat cheeses and place in an ovenproof dish. Bake for 5 minutes.

Remove from the oven and serve immediately.

Wine suggestion

Serve with a slightly fruity, medium-bodied white.

WHITE ROOT VEGETABLE SOUP WITH POPPY SEED BREAD

Serves 4
Preparation time: 10 minutes
Cooking time: 50 minutes

Ingredients
1 lb (500 g) white radishes
1 lb (500 g) Jerusalem artichokes
1 lb (500 g) parsnips
4 cups (1 liter) milk
2 slices poppy seed bread
Salt and pepper to taste

Peel and cube the white radishes, the Jerusalem artichokes, and the parsnips.

Pour the milk into a pot and add the vegetables. Add water to cover the vegetables. Bring to a boil, then lower the heat and simmer with the lid on for 40 minutes.

Preheat the oven to 200° F (100° C).

Cut the poppy seed bread into sticks and dry them out in the oven to make croutons.

Blend the soup thoroughly and then strain it. Season with salt and pepper.

Serve hot with the toasted bread fingers.

Baker's tip
If you don't have poppy seed bread, use a multigrain loaf.

Sandwiches
From Around
the World

SMOKED SALMON SUSHI, CUCUMBER, AND RADISH SPROUT SANDWICH

Serves 4
Preparation time: 20 minutes

In a bowl, mix the lemon juice, the cream cheese, and the chopped chives.

Spread this mixture on the slices of bread.

Ingredients

8 thin slices of turmeric bread,
crusts removed
½ cucumber
4 slices of smoked salmon
1 oz (25 g) radish sprouts
(available in organic food stores)

Wash the cucumber. Cut diagonally using a vegetable peeler to make long slivers. Place the cucumber slices on the bread. Arrange half a slice of smoked salmon over them. Add the radish sprouts. Roll up like a sushi and cover in plastic wrap.

Refrigerate until ready to serve.

For the chive sauce
Juice of 1 lemon
½ lb (250 g) cream cheese
A few sprigs of chives, chopped

Baker's tip

If you don't have turmeric or saffron bread, use a good quality sandwich loaf. In this case, add 1 ¾ teaspoons ground turmeric to the chive sauce. Instead of radish sprouts, you can use small arugula leaves.

TANDOORI CLUB SANDWICH

Serves 4
Preparation time: 20 minutes
Marinate for 1 hour
Cooking time: 20 minutes

Ingredients

10 oz (300 g) sweet potatoes or carrots
1 oz (20 g) black sesame seeds
(available in Asian grocery stores)
2 whole chicken breasts or 4 halves
12 slices sandwich loaf

For the marinade

1 ¼ cups (300 ml) whipping cream
10 oz mild, creamy goat cheese
3 tablespoons (25 g) ground turmeric
½ tablespoon (5 g) curry powder

Combine the ingredients for the marinade, then divide the mixture into 2 bowls.

Peel and grate the sweet potatoes (or the carrots). Add the sesame seeds.

Cut the chicken breasts in halves (if using whole breasts).
Place them in one of the bowls with the marinade, and the grated sweet potatoes or carrots in the other.
Refrigerate for 1 hour.

Toast the slices of sandwich loaf.

Preheat the oven to 350° F (180° F).
Cook the marinated chicken in an ovenproof dish for 15 minutes.

Slice the chicken finely.

Prepare the layers of the sandwich: start with the bread, then the grated potato, and finally the chicken. Make three layers. Cut each sandwich into 2 triangles.

Baker's tip
Accompany this sandwich with a nice crisp salad of arugula leaves.

MIDDLE EASTERN SANDWICH

Serves 4
Preparation time: 15 minutes
Cooking time: 15 minutes

Ingredients

2 eggplants
2 tablespoons (30 ml) olive oil
4 x ¼ lb (100 g) fougasses
1 Romaine lettuce
3 oz (80 g) slow-roasted tomatoes
2 teaspoons coarse salt
Pepper to taste

For the sauce

⅔ cup (100 g) plain yogurt
3 oz (100 g) feta

Combine the yogurt and the feta in a mixing bowl to make the sauce.

Preheat the oven to 425° F (210° C).

Wash the eggplants and cut them lengthways into 12 slices. Drizzle a little olive oil over them, and season with coarse salt and pepper. Line a baking tray with waxed paper and broil them in the oven for 15 minutes.

Wash and dry the lettuce leaves.
Cut the base of each fougasse so that they form pockets.

Spread the yogurt and feta sauce inside the fougasses. Cut the eggplant slices in half and fill the fougasses with the slow-roasted tomatoes, lettuce leaves, and the eggplant.

Baker's tip

You can also use pita bread.

PAN-FRIED SARDINES AND GRILLED PEPPER SANDWICH

Serves 4
Preparation time: 20 minutes
Cooking time: 25 minutes

Ingredients

4 red bell peppers
4 fresh sardines
2 tablespoons (30 ml) olive oil
2 buckwheat baguettes
1 bunch basil
Salt and pepper to taste

Preheat the oven to 425° F (210° C). Wash the bell peppers and broil them on a baking tray for 20 minutes. Peel them and remove the seeds. Set aside.

Gut the sardines and wash them. Fillet each fish. Pan-fry them for a few minutes in the olive oil. Season with salt and pepper.

Cut the buckwheat baguettes in the middle, then cut them lengthways, but without separating them into two. Put 2 sardine fillets, some grilled bell pepper, and a few basil leaves in each sandwich.

Baker's tip
You can use mackerel instead of sardines.

WHITE SAUSAGE, HONEY BREAD, AND EXOTIC FRUIT CHUTNEY

Serves 4
Preparation time: 20 minutes
Cooking time: 15 minutes

Ingredients
1 mango
1 pineapple
3 tablespoons (45 ml) grapeseed oil
Juice of 1 lime
1 teaspoon curry powder
4 white sausages (boudin blanc)
4 honey and olive oil rolls

Peel the mango and the pineapple. Cube the flesh.

Using half the oil, lightly fry the mango, the pineapple, the lime juice, and the curry powder until the mixture thickens. Set aside.

Fry the white sausages in the rest of the oil over medium heat until they are lightly colored all over.

Cut the rolls in half and insert a white sausage into each one.
Top with 2 tablespoons of mango-pineapple chutney.

Baker's tip
Instead of honey and olive oil rolls, serve with poppy seed baguette.

FOCACCIA WITH EGGPLANT, ZUCCHINI, AND TOMATOES

Serves 4
Preparation time: 20 minutes
Marinate for 20 minutes
Cooking time: 20 minutes

Ingredients
1 lb (500 g) eggplants
3 tablespoons (45 ml) olive oil
½ lb (250 g) cherry tomatoes
4 x 6 oz (180 g) fougasses
1 ½ oz (40 g) piece of Parmesan cheese
Salt and pepper to taste

For the zucchini marinade
2 zucchini
Juice of ½ lemon
2 tablespoons (30 ml) olive oil
1 tablespoon (15 ml) honey

Preheat the oven to 425° F (210° C).

Wash the eggplants. Broil them on a baking tray for 25 minutes. Peel them, then blend them with the olive oil, the salt, and the pepper. Set aside.

Wash the cherry tomatoes and cut them in half.

Wash the zucchini. Using a mandolin vegetable slicer or peeler, cut them into very fine slices. Combine the lemon juice, the olive oil, and the honey to make the marinade. Leave the sliced zucchini to marinate for 20 minutes.

Cut each fougasse lengthways in half and toast.

Spread the eggplant purée on the fougasses. Cover with the cherry tomatoes, the marinated zucchini slices, and a few slivers of Parmesan.

Wine suggestion
Serve with a well-chilled rosé.

ROAST CHICKEN IN BUCKWHEAT RUSTIC BREAD

Serves 4
Preparation time: 15 minutes
Marinate for 24 hours
Cooking time: 35 minutes

Ingredients

2 whole chicken breasts or 4 halves
½ cup (100 g) mayonnaise
1 lettuce
2 buckwheat baguettes
3 oz (80 g) dried tomatoes

For the marinade

3 tablespoons (50 ml) olive oil
3 tablespoons (50 ml) white wine
2 tablespoons (30 ml) soy sauce
Juice of ½ lemon
1 tablespoon (15 ml) Dijon mustard
1 bay leaf
1 sprig thyme
1 clove garlic, peeled and cut in half

A day ahead

Combine all the marinade ingredients in a mixing bowl.
Cut the chicken breasts in half. Marinate them for 24 hours in the fridge.

To prepare

Preheat the oven to 275° F (140° C).

Place the chicken in its marinade in an ovenproof dish. Cook for 15 minutes,
then increase the temperature to 350° F (180° C). Cook for a further 20 minutes.

Remove from the oven and leave to cool slightly. Slice it and pour the remaining marinade over, reserving 2 tablespoons (30 ml).
Strain the reserved marinade and leave to cool. Mix the strained marinade with the mayonnaise.

Wash and dry the lettuce leaves.

Cut each baguette into half, then slit the halves.
Spread the flavored mayonnaise on each side of the bread, and fill with a few lettuce leaves, the dried tomatoes, and the sliced chicken.

Baker's tip

If you cook the chicken a day ahead and leave it to marinate in the fridge, it will taste even better the next day.

100% PARISIAN

Serves 4
Preparation time: 10 minutes

Trim the mushroom stalks and wash the mushrooms well.
Process them in a food processor with the softened butter, the salt, and the pepper.

Cut the baguettes in half and slit them without separating them completely.

Ingredients

¼ lb (100 g) button mushrooms
½ cup (100 g) salted butter, softened
2 baguettes
8 slices cooked ham
4 slices Emmental cheese or similar
tasty hard cheese
Salt and pepper to taste

Spread the bread with the mushroom butter.

Insert 2 slices of ham and 1 slice of cheese in each.

Baker's tip

For a truly royal sandwich, add a few drops of truffle oil. At Kayser, choose the Monge baguettes, but if you're not near one of our bakeries, buy the best baguette you can.

BRIE CHEESE AND HAZELNUT BUTTER ON *PAIN VIENNOIS*

Serves 4
Preparation time: 10 minutes

Combine the softened butter and the hazelnuts.

Slit the *pain viennois*.

Ingredients

½ cup (100 g) salted butter, softened
¼ lb (100 g) grilled hazelnuts, chopped
4 *pains viennois* (Viennese bread)
16 slices of Brie cheese

Spread both sides of the sandwich with the hazelnut-butter mixture.

Place 4 slices of Brie in each sandwich.

Baker's tip

If you don't like the sweetness of *pain viennois*, replace it with a sesame baguette.

ERIC KAYSER'S FOIE GRAS CHEESEBURGER

Serves 4
Preparation time: 10 minutes
Cooking time: 10 minutes

Ingredients

5 fresh figs
1 ½ tablespoons (20 g) butter
1 tablespoon (15 ml) honey
Juice of ½ lemon
4 cheese rolls
½ lb (250 g) uncooked duck foie gras
Salt and pepper to taste

Wash the figs and cut them into quarters. Lightly fry them in the butter and honey.

Remove from heat and add the lemon juice.

Cut the cheese rolls in 2 and toast them.

Cut the foie gras into 4 slices. Season with salt and pepper, heat a frying pan, and sauté them 2 to 3 minutes on each side.

Insert a slice of foie gras and 5 fig quarters into each roll and close the burger.

Baker's tip

If you don't have cheese rolls, add a slice of a tasty hard cheese, such as Emmental, to the burger.

Breads for Dessert

CHOCOLATE SOUP
WITH BRIOCHE CROUTONS

Serves 4
Preparation time: 10 minutes
Cooking time: 15 minutes

Ingredients

1 cup (250 ml) whole milk
½ cup (125 ml) whipping cream
1 stick cinnamon
1 vanilla pod, slit lengthways
½ lb (250 g) dark chocolate
(70 percent cocoa)
6 oz (180 g) brioche

Pour the milk and the cream into a saucepan, and add the cinnamon stick and the slit vanilla pod to infuse. Bring to a boil and remove from heat. Remove the cinnamon and the vanilla pod.

Break up the chocolate into small pieces and add to the creamy mixture.
Whip it in thoroughly until the chocolate has melted and the mixture well combined, and set aside.
Heat the oven grill.

Slice the brioche and cut bite-sized discs with a cookie cutter.
Toast the brioche pieces under the grill until they turn a nice brown color, then place 4 toasted circles on each of 4 wooden skewers.

Warm the chocolate soup and pour it into soup bowls or glasses. Accompany with the brioche skewers.

Baker's tip

You can also enjoy this recipe with fresh fruit such as bananas, pears, etc.

CHOCOLATE ALMOND LOAF

Serves 8
Preparation time: 30 minutes
Baking time: 45 minutes

Ingredients

6 eggs
½ lb (250 g) almond paste, baking quality
½ lb (250 g) dark chocolate (70 percent cocoa)
⅓ cup (75 g) butter plus a little extra for the cake pan
½ cup (40 g) cake flour
2 teaspoons baking powder
5 oz (150 g) bittersweet hazelnut chocolate
2 oz (50 g) grilled pine nuts or almonds for decoration

8 inch (28–30 cm) loaf pan

In a food processor, mix the eggs, one by one, into the almond paste.
In a bain-marie, melt 5 oz (150 g) of the dark chocolate with the butter. Combine the melted chocolate with the almond paste, and then add the flour and the baking powder. Preheat the oven to 350° F (170° C) and butter the cake pan.

Melt the hazelnut chocolate in a bain-marie.
Pour half the cake mixture into the cake pan. Spoon in the melted hazelnut chocolate, then add the rest of the cake mixture.

Bake for 35 minutes until risen and cooked through.
Unmold the chocolate almond loaf and leave to cool on a wire rack. Melt the remaining 3 oz (100 g) of chocolate, ice the cake and decorate it with the pine nuts or almonds.

Baker's tip

Baking quality almond paste is 50 percent almonds and 50 percent sugar—you can buy it in specialty stores.

BREAD AND BUTTER PUDDING

Serves 4
Preparation time: 25 minutes
Baking time: 45 minutes

Ingredients

½ cup (125 ml) whole milk
½ cup (125 ml) heavy cream or crème
fraîche
1 vanilla pod, slit lengthways
3 eggs
½ cup (100 g) granulated sugar
¼ cup (50 g) unsalted butter, plus a little
for the cake pan
½ lb (200 g) sliced brioche
2 tablespoons confectioners' sugar
Fresh fruit for decoration

One ovenproof dish, 8 x 8 inches
(20 x 20 cm)

Pour the milk and the cream into a saucepan, and add the slit vanilla pod. Bring to a boil, stirring constantly. Remove from the heat and set aside to cool. Remove the vanilla pod.

Beat the eggs and the sugar together. When the cream-milk mixture has cooled, whip the eggs and sugar in.

Preheat the oven to 350° F (180° C) and butter an ovenproof dish.

Arrange the brioche slices in the bottom of the dish, overlapping them slightly. Pour the mixture over the brioche, and scatter knobs of butter on the top. Sprinkle with confectioners' sugar.

Place in a bain-marie and bake for about 40 minutes until golden brown. Remove from the oven and brown the top under the grill.

Transfer to a serving plate and decorate with fresh fruit.

Baker's tip
Sprinkle some extra sugar on the top before placing the pudding under the grill, so that it caramelizes like a crème brûlée.

FRENCH TOAST
WITH APPLES AND CUSTARD

Serves 4
Preparation time: 25 minutes
Baking time: 20 minutes

Ingredients

4 slices sourdough bread
3 Granny Smith apples
⅓ cup (80 g) butter
¼ cup (50 g) brown sugar

For the eggnog

4 egg yolks
2 whole eggs
1 cup (200 g) granulated sugar
2 cups (½ liter) whipping cream
3 tablespoons (45 ml) rum

For the custard

½ cup (125 ml) whole milk
½ vanilla pod, slit lengthways
2 egg yolks
2 tablespoons (25 g) granulated sugar

In a mixing bowl, prepare the eggnog: Beat the egg yolks with the whole eggs and the sugar. Mix in the cream and the rum.

Cut out circles of sourdough bread using a mold or a cookie cutter and dip them in the eggnog. Melt 2 tablespoons (30 g) butter in a frying pan and fry the bread over a medium heat until it turns golden on both sides. Keep in a warm place.

Peel the apples. Cut them in half and remove the cores. Cut each half into 4 pieces. Melt the remaining ¼ cup (50 g) butter in a frying pan. Pour in the brown sugar to make a caramel. Add the apples and cook them, turning them over, until they are brown all over. Keep warm.

To make the custard heat the milk with the slit vanilla pod in a saucepan so that the seeds infuse the milk. In a large bowl, beat the egg yolks together with the sugar until the texture thickens and turns pale. Pour the hot milk over the beaten egg yolks, beating constantly. Pour the mixture back into the saucepan, and, using a wooden spoon, stir constantly over medium heat until the custard coats the back of the spoon. It is essential that it doesn't come to a boil.

Place the warm slices of French toast on plates. Arrange the caramelized apples over them and pour the custard on top.

Baker's tip
For a completely different taste, try other types of bread.

SAUTÉED MIRABELLE PLUMS
WITH SAFFRON AND BREADSTICKS

Serves 4
Preparation time: 1 hour
Refrigeration time: 1 hour
Baking time: 30 minutes

Ingredients

10 oz (300 g) Mirabelle plums
1 ½ tablespoons (20 ml) butter
¼ cup (50 g) granulated sugar
5 threads saffron

For the breadstick dough
½ lb (250 g) bread flour
1 ½ teaspoons (6 g) granulated sugar
2 pinches salt
3 tablespoons (45 ml) olive oil
⅓ envelope (3 g) active dry yeast or
⅓ cake compressed fresh yeast
(6 g fresh yeast); dissolved
in 1 ½ tbs lukewarm water

In a mixing bowl, combine the flour, the sugar, the salt, and the olive oil.
Dilute the yeast in a little lukewarm water and add it to the other ingredients.
Pour in ½ cup (100 ml) cold water and knead until the ingredients form a smooth,
firm dough.
Refrigerate for 1 hour.

Preheat the oven to 200° F (100° C).
Roll the dough out to a thickness of just under ½ inch (1 cm). Cut strips ¼ inch (0.5 cm)
wide. Cover a baking tray with waxed paper and arrange the strips on this. Place a bowl of
water in the oven to maintain humidity. Bake for 15–20 minutes, until they are pale brown
in color.

Rinse the plums and remove the pits, leaving the fruit whole.
Melt the butter in a frying pan over a medium heat. Add the sugar and cook for a few
moments to make a light caramel sauce. Add the plums and cook them for 5 minutes. Stir
in the saffron threads.

 Arrange the fruit on serving plates and decorate with the breadsticks.

Baker's tip
The breadsticks can be replaced with slices of toasted baguette.

PEAR TRIFLE

Serves 8
Preparation time: 30 minutes
Baking time: 1 hour 25 minutes

Ingredients
¾ cup (200 ml) whole milk
3 eggs
½ cup (100 g) granulated sugar
¾ lb (350 g) brioche
4 pears
¼ cup (50 g) unsalted butter
1 vanilla pod, slit lengthways
Pepper
Juice of 1 lemon

For the caramel sauce
½ cup (100 ml) whipping cream
¼ cup (60 g) sugar
2 teaspoons (10 g) butter

One 10 inch (25 cm) charlotte mold

In a saucepan, heat the milk. In a mixing bowl, beat the eggs with ¼ cup (50g) sugar. Pour the hot milk into the mixing bowl, beating as you pour. Cut the brioche into cubes of about 1 inch (2 cm) and place in the liquid to soak for 2 minutes.

Peel three pears and cut them into cubes.

Melt the butter in a frying pan and add the pears, the remaining ¼ cup (50 g) sugar, and the slit vanilla pod to infuse the mixture with the seeds. Simmer for 5 minutes, stirring constantly. Sprinkle a little pepper into this.

Preheat the oven to 350° F (180° C).

Mix the cooked pears together with the brioche cubes.

Spoon the mixture into the mold, place in a bain-marie, and bake for an hour. Peel the remaining pear, cut it in half, and remove the core.

Using a vegetable peeler, cut thin, long slices of pear, and pour the lemon juice over. Unmold the trifle and decorate with these pear shavings.

To make the caramel sauce, bring the cream to a boil in a saucepan then remove from heat. In another saucepan, caramelize the sugar over a medium heat, stirring constantly. Add the butter and the boiled cream. Bring to a boil again and remove immediately from the heat.

Serve this sauce with the trifle.

Wine suggestion
Serve with a fine champagne.

BAKED PEACHES IN APRICOT JUICE WITH LEMON BREAD

Serves 4
Preparation time: 20 minutes
Baking time: 20 minutes

Ingredients

5 yellow peaches
¼ cup (50 g) butter
⅓ cup (75 g) granulated sugar
½ cup (100 ml) apricot juice
1 oz (25 g) chopped unsalted pistachios
for decoration
4 lemon breadrolls

One round cake pan, 8 inches
(20 cm) in diameter

Plunge the peaches into boiling water briefly and peel them. Cut them in half and remove the pits.
Melt the butter in a large frying pan. Add the sugar and make a light-colored caramel. Arrange 8 peach halves in the pan and simmer them lightly on each side. Remove the fruit with a skimmer and place them in the cake pan, leaving the caramel in the frying pan.

Preheat the oven to 400° F (200° C).
Cut the remaining 2 peach halves into small pieces and simmer gently in the pan with the caramel. Remove the pieces of peach to the cake pan, then deglaze the juices in the frying pan with the apricot juice and stir in 3 to 4 tablespoons water to form a smooth caramel. Pour the caramel over the peaches and cover the pan with aluminum foil.

Bake for 7–8 minutes. Use a blade or cake tester to check whether the peaches are soft. Remove the aluminum foil and continue baking. Allow the juices to reduce for about 5–6 minutes, basting the peaches regularly to caramelize them.

Decorate with the pistachios and serve immediately with the lemon breadrolls.

Baker's tip
If you don't have lemon breadrolls, serve this dessert with dried apricot bread.

SPICY TANGERINE SOUP
AND PISTACHIO *PAIN VIENNOIS*

Serves 4
Preparation time: 45 minutes
Resting time: 2 hours 30 minutes
Baking time: 35 minutes
Refrigeration: 6 hours

Ingredients

8 tangerines (keep the leaves
for decoration)
4 vanilla pods
Zest of 1 unwaxed tangerine
1 cup (200 g) granulated sugar
3 cinnamon sticks
4 star anise
1 ¾ teaspoons black peppercorns

For the pistachio *pain viennois*
(Viennese bread)
2 ½ cups (250 g) bread flour
1 pinch of salt
⅓ envelope (2.5 g) active dry yeast or
⅓ cake compressed fresh yeast
(5 g fresh yeast); dissolved
in 4 tsp lukewarm water
1 ¾ tablespoons granulated sugar
3 tablespoons (45 g) butter
1 ½ tablespoons powdered milk
2 ½ tablespoons (40 ml) whipping cream
1 oz (25 g) pistachio paste
(buy online or at finer grocery stores)
1 oz (25 g) whole, unsalted pistachios
½ cup (125 ml) water

Pour all the ingredients for the *pain viennois* into the bowl of a food processor.
Knead for 5 minutes at low speed and for 8 minutes at high speed.
Cover the dough with a damp cloth and allow to rest for 30 minutes.
Divide the dough into ½ lb (250 g) portions. Form into loaves 12 inches (30 cm) long
and leave them to stand at room temperature for 2 hours, covered with a damp cloth.
Preheat the oven to 325° F (160° C) for 10 minutes.
Line a baking pan with waxed paper and bake the loaves for 25 minutes.
Peel the tangerines, and use a small, sharp knife to remove the pith, leaving the
tangerines whole.
Insert ½ vanilla pod into each tangerine.

In a saucepan, pour 4 cups (1 liter) water, add the sugar, the cinnamon sticks,
the tangerine zest, the star anise, and the peppercorns. Bring to a boil and simmer
for 3 minutes. Add the tangerines and cook them for about 1 minute. Remove from heat
and allow the contents of the saucepan to cool together so the flavors can meld.
Refrigerate for about 6 hours.

Arrange the tangerines in a serving bowl, add the syrup, and decorate with
the tangerine leaves. Serve with the pistachio *pain viennois*.

Baker's tip

The next morning, butter the leftover bread to enjoy with your coffee.

CHESTNUT FLAN, SWEET CHESTNUT LOAF, AND TANGERINE COULIS

Serves 4
Preparation time: 30 minutes
Baking time: 30 minutes
Refrigeration: 6 hours

Ingredients

2 eggs
¼ cup (50 g) granulated sugar
3 ½ tablespoons (20 g) flour
½ cup (100 ml) whole milk
½ cup (100 ml) whipping cream
5 oz (150 g) chestnut cream (you can find this at finer grocery stores)
1 chestnut loaf

For the tangerine coulis

Juice and zest of 1 unwaxed tangerine
1 ¾ tablespoons (20 g) granulated sugar
1 sheet (2 g) leaf gelatin

Four ramekins or one 8 inch (20 cm) diameter pan

Preheat the oven to 350° F (180° C).

In a mixing bowl, beat the eggs and the sugar together, and then incorporate the flour. Bring the milk and the cream to a boil in a saucepan and mix in the chestnut cream. Remove from heat, and pour over the egg mixture, mixing thoroughly.

Pour the mixture into a cake pan and place the pan in a bain-marie. Bake for about 20 minutes in the oven or until a cake tester or sharp knife comes out dry.

In a saucepan, bring the juice, the sugar, and the zest to a boil. Remove from heat. Soak the gelatin leaf in cold water for a few minutes. Wring out the water and dissolve the leaf in the hot liquid. Refrigerate for 6 hours.

Toast the slices of chestnut loaf. Arrange the chestnut flan on a serving plate. Decorate it with the toast and pour over the tangerine coulis.

Baker's tip

Instead of chestnut bread, you can use buckwheat bread.

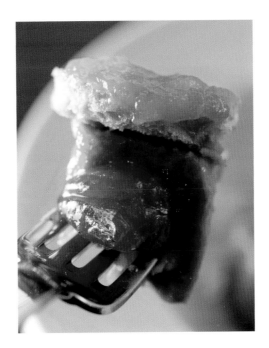

BAKED PERSIMMONS WITH DARK CHOCOLATE OPEN SANDWICHES

Serves 4
Preparation time: 15 minutes
Baking time: 20 minutes

Ingredients

1 cup (200 g) granulated sugar
1 ⅓ cup (300 ml) passion fruit juice
4 persimmons
½ cup (100 ml) water
½ lb (200 g) sourdough bread

For the dark chocolate cream

7 oz (200 g) dark chocolate (70 percent cocoa)
¾ cup (200 ml) whipping cream
1 ½ tablespoons (20 g) butter

Cook the sugar over a medium heat, stirring constantly, until it turns a caramel color. Incorporate the passion fruit juice and set aside.
Preheat the oven to 350° F (170° C).

Wash the persimmons, cut them in half, and arrange them in an ovenproof dish.
Add the caramel sauce and the water.
Place in the oven and cook for 30 minutes, basting the fruit frequently with the caramel-juice mixture.

Check the texture of the persimmons with a sharp knife—they should be soft.
Break the chocolate into small pieces. In a saucepan, bring the cream to a boil. Remove from the heat, and add the chocolate. Stir until dissolved and incorporate the butter.

Slice the bread and toast it. Spread with the chocolate cream and serve with the baked persimmons.

Baker's tip
Instead of persimmons, you can use papaya.

STRAWBERRIES IN WINE WITH PINK CARAMELIZED ALMOND BREAD

Serves 8
Preparation time: 45 minutes
Resting time: 2 hours 30 minutes
Baking time: 35 minutes

Ingredients

10 oz (300 g) strawberries
⅓ cup (75 ml) red wine
⅓ cup (75 g) granulated sugar
2 black peppercorns
2 cloves
1 cinnamon stick
1 vanilla pod, slit lengthways

For the pink caramelized almond bread

2 ½ cups (250 g) bread flour
1 pinch of salt
⅓ envelope (2.5 g) active dry yeast or
⅓ cake compressed fresh yeast
(5 g fresh yeast); dissolved
in 4 tsp lukewarm water
1 ¾ tablespoons (20 g) granulated sugar
3 tablespoons (45 g) butter
1 ½ tablespoons (10 g) powdered milk
1 tablespoon (20 ml) whipping cream
½ cup (125 ml) water
2 ½ oz (75 g) pink caramelized almonds

Place all the ingredients for the bread, except the caramelized almonds, in the bowl of a food processor. Knead for 5 minutes at low speed and then 8 minutes at high speed. Add the caramelized almonds, kneading them in by hand. Set aside the dough to rest for 30 minutes, covered with a damp cloth.

Divide the dough into ½ lb (250 g) portions.

Make loaves about 12 inches long (30 cm). Leave to rest at room temperature for 2 hours, covered with a damp cloth.

Line a baking tray with waxed paper and preheat the oven to 325° F (160° C). Bake the loaves for 25 minutes.

Wash the strawberries and cut them into quarters. Bring the red wine to a boil and flambé it. Add the other ingredients to the liquid and allow to simmer. Add the strawberries and simmer further. Remove from heat and allow the flavors of the ingredients to blend.

Spoon the mixture into soup bowls and add the cubes of pink caramelized almond bread.

Wine suggestion
Serve with a sparkling red wine, such as Lambrusco.

CHOCOLATE-PRALINE OPEN SANDWICHES WITH HAZELNUT CARAMEL SLIVERS

Serves 8
Preparation: 45 minutes
Resting time: 2 hours 30 minutes
Baking time: 35 minutes

Ingredients

¾ cup (200 ml) whipping cream
3 oz (100 g) praline paste (you can buy this at specialty grocery stores)
7 oz (200 g) dark chocolate (70 percent cocoa)
7 oz (200 g) whole hazelnuts
2 teaspoons (10 ml) water
2 tablespoons (25 g) granulated sugar
2 teaspoons (10 g) butter

For the *pain viennois*

2 ½ cups (250 g) bread flour
⅓ envelope (2.5 g) active dry yeast or ⅓ cake compressed fresh yeast, (5 g fresh yeast); dissolved in 4 tsp lukewarm water
1 ¾ tablespoons (20 g) granulated sugar
3 tablespoons (45 g) butter
1 ½ tablespoons (10 g) powdered milk
¾ cup (200 ml) whipping cream
2 ½ oz (75 g) praline paste
1 pinch salt
½ cup (125 ml) water

Place all the ingredients for the *pain viennois* in the bowl of a food processor. Knead for 5 minutes at low speed and then 8 minutes at high speed.

Leave the dough to rest for 30 minutes, covered with a damp cloth.
Divide the dough into ½ lb (250 g) portions.

Form loaves about 12 inches long (30 cm).

Leave to rest at room temperature for 2 hours, covered with a damp cloth.

Preheat the oven to 325° C (160° F), then bake the loaves for 25 minutes.
Remove from the oven and leave to cool slightly before cutting in two lengthways.

While the bread is baking, prepare the praline ganache.

Heat the cream in a saucepan. Remove from heat and incorporate the praline paste and then the dark chocolate. Set aside to cool.

Grill the hazelnuts in the oven.

Make a caramel using the water and the sugar. Mix in the hot hazelnuts. Finally, add the butter to decrease the sticky texture. Pour the mixture on waxed paper and set aside to cool.

When the bread is toasted, spread the praline ganache over the slices.

Decorate with slivers of the hazelnut caramel mixture.

Baker's tip

If you're making this for children, use chocolate-hazelnut spread (such as Nutella) instead of ganache.

STRAWBERRY CLUB SANDWICH

Serves 4
Preparation time: 15 minutes
Cooking time: 5 minutes

Ingredients

8 slices of sandwich loaf
½ lb (250 g) raspberry jelly
10 oz (300 g) strawberries
3 oz (100 g) raspberries
2 oz (50 g) bunches of red currants for decoration
1 ½ tablespoons (20 g) butter
2 ½ tablespoons (30 g) sugar

Remove the crusts from the sandwich loaf slices and toast the bread. Set aside to cool.

Spread the raspberry jelly over the toast and sandwich 4 slices together. Cut the sandwiches in half to form triangles.

Arrange on plates.

Wash the fruit, and cut the strawberries in half. Melt the butter in a frying pan over medium heat. Add the sugar, then the strawberries. Cook gently for 2 minutes, remove from the heat, and add the raspberries. Mix through delicately so as not to crush the raspberries.

Arrange the fruit next to the club sandwich, and decorate with the bunches of red currants.

Baker's tip

The recipe is better if you use homemade jelly that is not too sweet—less than 50 percent sugar.

BAKED CINNAMON-FLAVORED PEARS WITH WHITE CHOCOLATE BREAD

Serves 4
Preparation time: 15 minutes
Baking time: 25 minutes

Ingredients

½ cup (100 g) granulated sugar
2 tablespoons (30 g) butter
¾ cup (200 ml) whipping cream
2 cinnamon sticks
4 pears
1 pain viennois with white chocolate chips

Caramelize the sugar by cooking over a medium heat, stirring constantly, until it turns a golden color. Mix in the butter. Add the cream and the cinnamon sticks. As soon as the mixture comes to the simmer, remove it from the heat. Preheat the oven to 350° F (180° C).

Peel the pears and place them in an ovenproof dish.

Pour the hot caramel sauce, including the cinnamon sticks, over them. Add ¼ cup (50 ml) water and bake for 15–20 minutes, basting the pears frequently. Use a sharp knife or cake tester to see whether they are baked.

Slice the white chocolate bread and toast it.

When the pears are baked, arrange them on plates. Pour the caramel sauce from the dish over them and decorate with the slices of toast.

Baker's tip

If you don't have white chocolate bread, use a brioche and small pieces of white chocolate.

WARM CHOCOLATE EGGS
AND COCOA BREAD FINGERS

Serves 8
Preparation time: 30 minutes
Baking time: 4 minutes

Ingredients

8 eggs
½ cup (100 g) butter
¼ lb (115 g) dark chocolate
(70 percent cocoa)
⅔ cup (130 g) granulated sugar
⅔ cup (60 g) flour
1 x 5 oz (150 g) cocoa loaf

A day ahead

Remove the tops of the eggs using an egg topper. Empty the eggs, setting aside the contents of 2 whole eggs in one bowl, and 2 yolks in another. Soak the shells in hot water. Remove the inner membrane and leave the shells overnight to dry upside down on a dishcloth.

Melt the butter and the chocolate in a bain-marie. In a mixing bowl, beat the 2 whole eggs, the 2 yolks, and the sugar. Then mix in the flour. Combine the mixture with the melted chocolate and butter. Refrigerate overnight.

To prepare

Preheat the oven to 350° F (180° C).
Fill the eggshells three-quarters full with the chocolate mixture and place in an ovenproof dish.

Cut the cocoa bread into small fingers.

Bake the eggs for 4 minutes.

Remove the eggs from the oven, put them in egg cups, and serve with the bread fingers.

Baker's tip
You can substitute fresh fruit for bread fingers.

GINGERBREAD MILLE-FEUILLE

Serves 4
Preparation time: 30 minutes
Baking time: 20 minutes
Refrigeration: 2 hours

Ingredients

10 oz (300 g) dark chocolate
(70 percent cocoa)
Zest of 1 unwaxed lemon
2 tablespoons (30 ml) whole milk
½ cup (130 ml) whipping cream
⅓ cup (75 g) butter
4 egg whites
1 ¾ tablespoons (20 g) granulated sugar
12 slices gingerbread

In a bain-marie, melt the chocolate together with the lemon zest.
In a saucepan, bring the milk and the cream to a boil, and pour the liquid into the melted chocolate, mixing well. Dice 1 ½ tablespoons (25 g) of the butter and whip it into the mixture.

Beat the egg whites stiffly, adding the sugar by thirds. Spoon one third of the beaten egg whites into the chocolate and mix in. Gently fold in the rest of the beaten egg whites. Refrigerate the mixture for 2 hours.

In a frying pan, melt the rest of the butter. Pour it over the gingerbread slices. Toast under the oven grill. Set aside to cool.

When it is quite cool, sandwich the gingerbread together with the chocolate mousse, making 3 or 4 layers.

Your mille-feuille is ready to serve.

Baker's tip
This is good with custard or a scoop of your favorite ice cream.

OPEN PISTACHIO CREAM SANDWICHES AND EXOTIC FRUIT

Serves 4
Preparation time: 30 minutes
Resting time: 1 hour
Baking time: 15 minutes

Ingredients

2 mangoes
3 tablespoons (50 ml) lemon juice
¼ cup (50 g) butter
5 tablespoons (100 g) honey
2 passion fruit
½ lb (200 g) sourdough bread
Freshly ground black pepper

For the pistachio cream

½ cup (125 ml) whole milk
1 ½ tablespoons (10 g) pistachio paste
(buy online or at specialty stores)
3 egg yolks
2 tablespoons (25 g) granulated sugar
1 ½ tablespoons (15 g) cornstarch
½ cup (100 ml) whipping cream
3 ½ teaspoons (10 g)
confectioners' sugar

Peel the mangoes. Working round the pit, cut the flesh into cubes. Macerate them in the lemon juice for an hour in the refrigerator.

To make the pistachio cream, heat the milk in a saucepan with the pistachio paste. Remove from heat when thoroughly blended.

Whip the egg yolks with the sugar until the mixture becomes pale yellow.
Stir in the cornstarch. Blend a little boiling milk into this mixture, and then pour it all back into the saucepan. Bring it back to the simmer, stirring constantly. Leave to cool in the refrigerator.

Cool the beaters of the electric egg beater in the refrigerator. Add the confectioners' sugar to the cream and whip stiffly. Gently fold 3 oz (100 g) of the whipped cream into the cool pistachio cream.

Toast the slices of bread in the oven and crush a few of them to make crumbs.
Melt the butter in a frying pan. Pour the honey into the pan and caramelize it.
Fry the mango cubes very lightly in the caramel, being careful that they retain their shape.

Add the passion fruit seeds and give two twists of the pepper grinder over the mixture.
Spread the toast with pistachio cream and add the fruit. Sprinkle with the toasted breadcrumbs.

Wine suggestion
Serve with a full-bodied, sweet white wine.

CHOCOLATE FLOATING ISLANDS
WITH CRUNCHY HAZELNUT BREAD

Serves 4
Preparation time: 30 minutes
Baking time: 10 minutes

In a saucepan, bring the milk to a boil with the cinnamon and the vanilla pod. Remove from heat. Break the chocolate into pieces and incorporate it into the milk. Leave the flavors of the ingredients to blend.

Ingredients

1 cup (250 ml) whole milk
1 cinnamon stick
1 vanilla pod
7 oz (200 g) dark chocolate (70 percent cocoa)
4 egg whites
¼ cup (50 g) granulated sugar
½ lb (230 g) hazelnut bread
A good pinch of salt
Cocoa powder for decoration

Add the sugar to the egg whites and beat stiffly.
Boil salted water in a saucepan.

Using 2 teaspoons, form the egg whites into small balls. Poach them in the simmering water for 1 to 2 minutes each side.

Drain them on paper towel. Slice the hazelnut bread and toast it.

Remove the cinnamon stick and the vanilla pod from the melted chocolate mixture. Spoon the chocolate mixture into soup plates. Gently place the egg whites in this and decorate with the hazelnut bread and a sprinkle of cocoa powder.

Baker's tip

Sprinkle the floating islands lightly with cocoa powder.

A CUP OF STRONG VIENNESE COFFEE WITH TOASTED CROUTONS

Serves 4
Preparation time: 35 minutes
Refrigeration: 6 hours

Ingredients

First layer

2 sheets (4 g) leaf gelatin
½ cup strong coffee (espresso or
brewed, if possible)

Second layer

1 cup (250 ml) whole milk
¾ cup (40 g) instant coffee granules
4 egg yolks
⅓ cup (60 g) granulated sugar
2 ½ tablespoons (25 g) cornstarch
3 sheets (6 g) leaf gelatin
½ cup (125 ml) whipping cream

Third layer

1 cup (250 ml) crème fraîche
or heavy cream
2 tablespoons (25 g) granulated sugar

4 slices sandwich loaf
A little melted chocolate
or cocoa powder for decoration

4 glasses

First layer

Soak the 2 leaves of gelatin in cold water and when they are soft, wring them out.
In a saucepan, heat the coffee and dissolve the gelatin leaves in it.
Pour out into 4 glasses and refrigerate for about 6 hours.

Second layer

In a saucepan, bring the milk and the instant coffee granules to a boil.
Remove from heat. In a mixing bowl, beat the egg yolks, the sugar, and the cornstarch until the mixture turns pale. Pour a little hot milk over this, continuing to beat, and pour it all back into the saucepan. Bring slowly to a simmer, stirring constantly.

Soak 3 leaves of gelatin in cold water and when they are soft, wring out the water. Stir them into the instant coffee mixture. Cover the saucepan with plastic wrap and refrigerate.

When it is cool, beat the whipping cream until firm and gently fold it into the mixture. Spoon the coffee cream over the coffee jelly and put back in the refrigerator.

Third layer

Stiffly whip the crème fraîche with the sugar.
Dice the sandwich loaf slices into small cubes. Brown them lightly in the oven. Set aside.

Remove the glasses from the refrigerator and top with the whipped cream. Arrange the croutons lightly on top. You can drizzle with melted chocolate or sprinkle a little cocoa powder to decorate.

Baker's tip

Add a little rum to the coffee jelly or to the frothy cream.

TOASTED FIG BREAD WITH FRESH FRUIT AND RASPBERRY COULIS

Serves 4
Preparation time: 15 minutes

Ingredients

1 fig loaf
¼ lb (125 g) raspberries
½ lb (250 g) strawberries
10 fresh figs
½ tablespoon (10 g) confectioners' sugar
½ lb (250 g) apricot preserve

Preheat the oven to 350° F (180° C). Cut the fig loaf lengthways and toast it in the oven. Set aside.

Wash the fruit. Blend the raspberries to make a coulis and strain the liquid. Mix in the confectioners' sugar. Set aside.

Hull the strawberries and cut them into quarters. Cut the figs into 8.

Arrange the assortment of strawberries and figs on the toasted bread, overlapping the pieces. Warm the apricot preserve and glaze the fruit while this is still liquid.

Decorate with the raspberry coulis.

Baker's tip

Serve this dessert with mint sherbet.

SPICED PINEAPPLE
IN A COCONUT BRIOCHE

Serves 6
Preparation time: 30 minutes
Baking time: 2 hours 10 minutes
Resting time: 2 hours

Ingredients

For the baked pineapple

⅔ cup (125 g) granulated sugar
1 vanilla pod, slit lengthways
1 banana
4 slices of fresh ginger
2 cups (½ liter) water
1 small whole pineapple

For the coconut brioche

2 ½ cups (250 g) bread flour
3 ½ tablespoons (40 g) sugar
1 teaspoon (5 g) salt
1 envelope (7.5 g) active dry yeast or
1 cake compressed fresh yeast
(15 g fresh yeast); dissolved
in ¼ cup lukewarm water
2 whole eggs and 1 egg yolk
1 ⅓ cups (100 g) shredded coconut
3 ½ tablespoons (45 ml) water
⅔ cup (150 g) unsalted butter, softened

A day ahead

Pour the sugar into a saucepan and add the vanilla pod. Cook over a medium heat until the sugar forms a golden caramel.

Slice the banana into circles. Add them to the caramel, together with the ginger, and leave for the flavors to blend. Slowly pour the water into the caramel and bring to a boil. Blend and strain.

Preheat the oven to 400° F (210° C).
Peel the pineapple taking care to remove the eyes, leaving it whole. Place it on a baking tray, pour over the caramel sauce and bake for an hour, basting frequently.

The pineapple is ready when the blade of a knife can easily be pushed into the flesh. Remove from the oven, set aside to cool, and refrigerate.

Prepare the brioche dough:
In the bowl of a food processor, combine the flour, the sugar, the salt, the yeast, the 2 whole eggs, and the coconut. Knead at low speed, then increase the speed, gradually adding the water. Continue kneading until the texture is homogeneous. Add the softened butter and knead again for 5 minutes.
Cover with a damp cloth and refrigerate overnight.

To assemble

Roll out the dough.
Place the pineapple in the center and wrap it completely in the dough, sealing it at the top so that it doesn't come unstuck while baking. Leave the dough to rise at room temperature, uncovered, for about 2 hours.

Preheat the oven to 325° F (160° C).
Use a pastry brush to baste the brioche with the egg yolk and bake for about 40 minutes.

Serve hot.

What Makes a Good Bread?

There are, of course, objective criteria that will allow you to distinguish between superior and inferior quality bread. In France, bakery-made bread has always been an integral part of the meal, and even though baguettes are also produced in factories, they don't bear comparison to the breads made by bakers using age-old traditions. This is what we would like you to enjoy. That being said, we often forget that the criteria for appreciating bread are matters of personal taste, upbringing, and circumstances.

Recognizing an Inferior Bread

Inferior bread often simply doesn't look appetizing. Its color is usually pale and the crust lacks sheen. It doesn't have that strong baked smell so characteristic of traditionally made bread. When you hold it, you can feel it lacks elasticity. Under a little pressure, a browned crust won't crackle, and if it's less well baked, the bread won't regain its original form. When you taste it, the soft part, known as the crumb, is mealy and dissolves very quickly when it comes into contact with your tongue. Even the initially weak taste doesn't linger long.

The Right Words for Bread

So that we could express the sensations we feel when eating good bread, we decided to organize a bread tasting along the lines of a wine tasting. I should point out that all the breads we tasted were from Kayser bakeries, and all the participants we invited work with fine foods and wines. All agreed that the breads looked and smelled good. Some mentioned aromas of toast and coffee, while others described the smells of flour and hazelnut. The interior of each bread was light yet firm. The thickness of the crusts depended on the type of bread, and was either crackly or crisp. What differed the most was each taster's personal preferences and the enjoyment derived from the breads. In addition to tasting the breads, our participants explained what, for them, is the perfect bread.

light

crackle

dense

A Description of the Products we Tasted, all of them Made According to French Baking Traditions

crunch

The Baguette
COLOR: lovely golden color, flecked with small toasted patches.
AROMA: toast, hazelnut.
SOUND: fine but crisp crust.
TASTE: the crumb has a lovely texture, and the bread has long finish.
FOOD PAIRING: butter, preserves, or to accompany a meal.

Sourdough Bread (also called Rustic Bread)
COLOR: a bread that looks good, appetizing, with a light, generous crumb.
AROMA: rather strong aroma of toast. Some tasters were reminded of the bread they ate as children.
SOUND: crunches rather than crackles.
TASTE: the crust only makes up a small part of this bread, and crumb is more acidic than the baguette.
FOOD PAIRING: everyone agreed that this a bread to eat with vegetable soup.

crust

grilled

Buckwheat Bread

COLOR: this rustic-looking bread is slightly gray.

AROMA: pronounced warm smell of Breton buckwheat crêpe.

SOUND: crunchier than the sourdough bread.

TASTE: the texture is light yet dense. It has good acidity. Even though its taste is more pronounced than that of the sourdough bread, it's a bread that goes down well.

FOOD PAIRING: fresh goat cheese, smoked fish.

Rye Bread

COLOR: the tasters found this darker bread very appetizing.

AROMA: very complex, with aromas of honey, toast, and strong coffee.

SOUND: very crunchy. It appears to have been baked for a considerable time in the oven.

TASTE: a denser bread. Well toasted, with slight bitterness set off by the sweetness of honey flavors.

FOOD PAIRING: a little salted butter and oysters.

honey
golden

coffee

Walnut Bread
COLOR: the walnut loaf is smaller and very smooth. The walnuts almost pop through the crust.
AROMA: mouthwatering buttery aromas mixed with walnut.
SOUND: its melt-in-the-mouth quality means that it doesn't make much sound when eaten.
TASTE: the soft brioche-type texture brings out the crunchiness of the walnuts.
FOOD PAIRING: it can be eaten on its own, but goes well with a fruity hard cheese such as a French Jura and a glass of after-dinner wine.

Brioche
COLOR: golden with some darker color.
AROMA: melted butter.
TASTE: buttery puff pastry, creamy egg desserts. Very delicate and light.
FOOD PAIRING: a fine champagne, dark chocolate

butter

appetizing

acidity

mouth-watering

hazelnut

melting

157

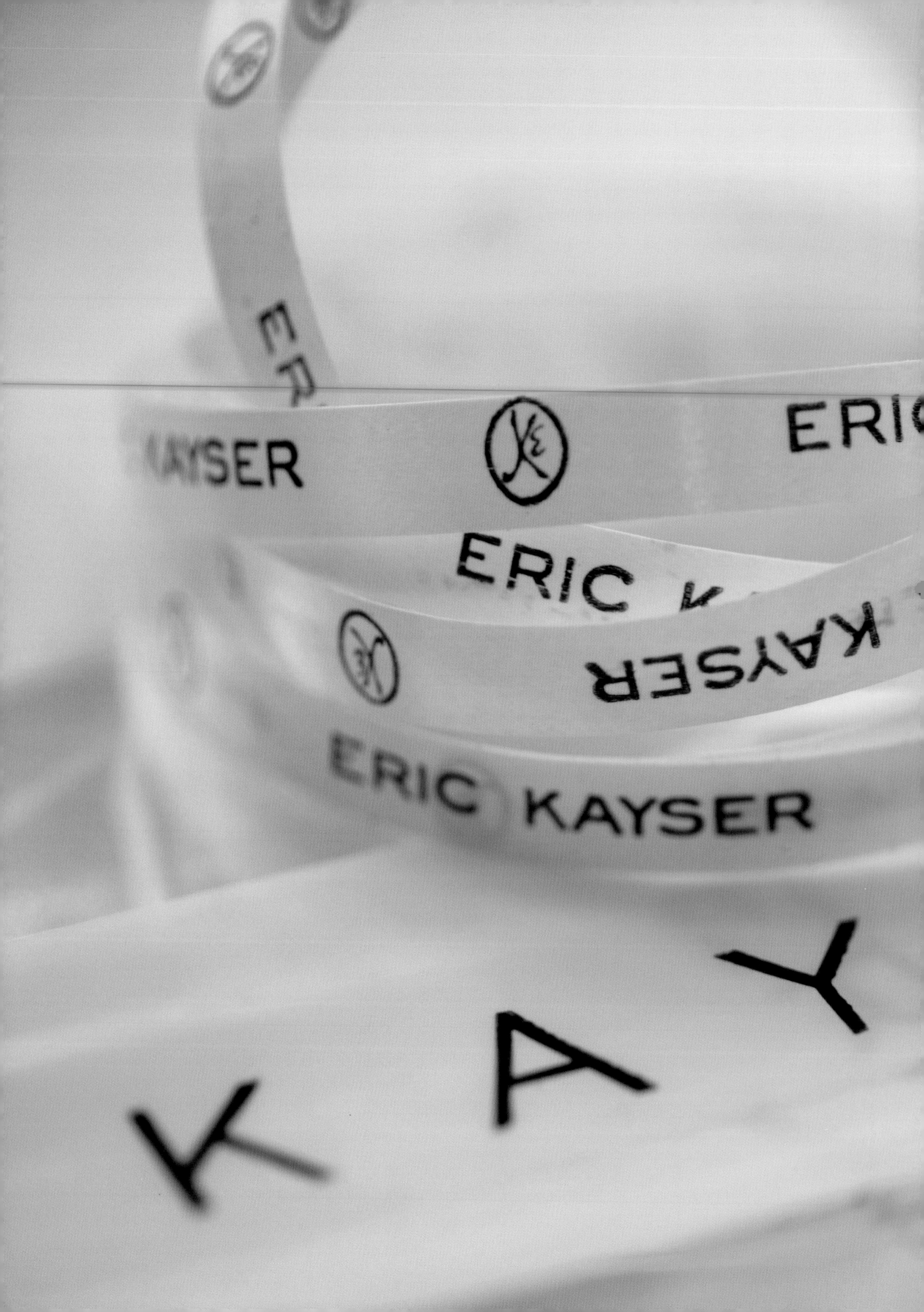
KAYSER
ERIC
ERIC
KAYSER
ERIC KAYSER
KAY

KAYSER

ER

®

S E R

Acknowledgments

I dedicate this book to Laurence, my wife, and to Alexis and Tanguy, my children, who make me happy to wake up each morning.

I am very grateful to all the members of the team who helped me create this book: Franck Colombié, pastry chef; Yaïr Yosefi, chef; and Julien Desrée, head baker. Thanks also to the wine club members who tasted the breads: Olivier Schvirtz, Massimo Berti, Didier Bocquet, Gaël Chauvet, Amélie Gamet, Sharon Bar-cochva, Merav Kane-Yosefi, and Yair Haidu.

As well as to our suppliers:
Deroche
M. Khaled
Pasta Linea
Hugo Desnoyer
Ercuis & Raynaud